In Trousers

by

William Finn

SAMUEL FRENCH, INC.

45 WEST 25TH STREET   NEW YORK 10010
7623 SUNSET BOULEVARD   HOLLYWOOD 90046
LONDON   *TORONTO*

PROMENADE THEATRE

Under the direction of Ben Sprecher

Roger Berlind   Franklin R. Levy   Gregory Harrison

present

by

William Finn

starring

Stephen Bogardus   Catherine Cox
Kathy Garrick   Sherry Hursey

Setting by
Santo Loquasto

Lighting by
Marilyn Rennagel

Costumes by
Madeline Ann Graneto

Musical Direction by
Roy Leake, Jr.

Orchestrations by
Michael Starobin

Sound by
Tom Morse

Casting by
Julie Hughes & Barry Moss

Directed by

Matt Casella

An earlier version of the musical was produced at Playwrights Horizons in 1978.

CAST

Marvin .... STEPHEN BOGARDUS

The Ladies

His wife .... CATHERINE COX

His high school sweetheart .... SHERRY HURSEY

His teacher, Miss Goldberg
(who always wears sunglasses) .... KATHY GARRICK

UNDERSTUDIES

Understudies never substitute for listed players unless a specific announcement for the appearance is made at the time of the performance.
Wife and Sweetheart—Carol Dilley; Miss Goldberg—Mary Bond Davis.

MUSICIANS

Sande Campbell—piano; Laurie A. Frink—trumpet; John Harvey—drums; Robert J. Magnuson — woodwinds; Ralph Olsen — woodwinds; Edward S. Strauss — synthesizers; Orchestra Contractor — Seymour Red Press.

In Trousers opened Off-Broadway at the Promenade Theatre on March 26, 1985.

MUSICAL NUMBERS

In Trousers (the dream)

I can't sleep .... Marvin and the ladies
Time to wake up .... His wife
I have a family .... Marvin
How Marvin eats his breakfast .... Marvin and the ladies
Marvin's giddy seizures 1 .... His high school sweetheart
My high school sweetheart .... High school sweetheart and everyone
Set those sails .... Miss Goldberg and the ladies
I swear I won't ever again .... Marvin
High school ladies at five o'clock ... High school sweetheart and the ladies
The rape of Miss Goldberg .... Marvin and Miss Goldberg
Love me for what I am .... Marvin and his wife
I am wearing a hat .... High school sweetheart and Miss Goldberg
Wedding song .... Everyone
Three seconds .... Marvin
How the body falls apart .... The ladies
I feel him slipping away .... His wife and the ladies
Whizzer going down .... Marvin
Marvin's giddy seizures 2 .... Everyone
I'm breaking down .... His wife
Packing up .... Marvin
Breakfast over sugar .... Marvin and his wife
How America got its name .... High school sweetheart,
Miss Goldberg and Marvin

Time to wake up (reprise) .... His wife
Another sleepless night .... Everyone
Goodnight/No hard feelings .... Marvin, his wife,
his high school sweetheart and Miss Goldberg

IN TROUSERS *IS PERFORMED WITHOUT AN INTERMISSION.*

6

AUTHOR'S NOTE

Directors of any ability will see in this show a chance to have a wonderful time. Do what you want. Just don't overburden the show with a huge, unwieldly set. And keep it clean. And keep it cool so it doesn't come off as some yuppie kvetching. Otherwise, I'm sure you'll do a decent job.

On the record album of an earlier version of this show, I wrote: "So Marvin grows up (after a fashion), says goodbye to the ladies (more to the point), and learns to live with always getting what he wants." But alot of the material was about my learning to write the kind of show songs I want to write. So the show is about Marvin's education, and mine.

William Finn
April 20, 1986

Special thanks to:

André Bishop
Alison Fraser
Robin Goodman
Ginny Read
Howard Rosenstone
Caroll Rothman
Arthur Salvadore
Ron Spivak
Michael Starobin
Mary Testa
and *Ira Weitzman*

for my parents

In Trousers

IN TROUSERS (1)

LADIES.
MARVIN, MARVIN,
MARVIN,
MAR . . . VIN

MARVIN.
THE MAN IS DREAMING IN TROUSERS
LAUGHING IN TROUSERS
PLAYING IN TROUSERS
MAKING MUSIC IN TROUSERS
MAKING MOVIES IN TROUSERS
FIGHTING IN TROUSERS
SINGING AND DANCING AND
  WRITING IN TROUSERS
MARVIN IS WAITING IN TROUSERS
HE IS CRYING IN TROUSERS
HE IS LIVING IN TROUSERS
MARVIN'S SCREWING IN TROUSERS
IN TROUSERS. IN TROUSERS.
IN TROUSERS.
IN TROUSERS.

LADIES.
MARVIN'S GIDDY SEIZURES.
MARVIN NEEDS LOVE.   MARVIN.
HE NEEDS LOVE.   IN TROUSERS.
HE NEEDS LOVE.
HE NEEDS LOVE.
HE NEEDS LOVE.

MARVIN'S GIDDY SEIZURES.
MARVIN NEEDS LOVE.   MARVIN.
HE NEEDS LOVE.   IN TROUSERS.
HE NEEDS LOVE.
HE NEEDS LOVE.
HE NEEDS LOVE.

AHHH . . .

9

I CAN'T SLEEP (2)

LADIES.
MARVIN'S GIDDY SEIZURES.
MARVIN NEEDS LOVE.
HE NEEDS LOVE.
HE NEEDS LOVE.
HE NEEDS LOVE.
HE NEEDS LOVE.
HE NEEDS LOVE.
HE NEEDS LOVE.
  MARVIN.
AHHH!
  LADIES.
HE NEEDS LOVE.

(*MARVIN dreams of men who turn out to be women.*)

(*At the beginning of this song the LADIES are dressed as men
    in pants and fedoras or whatever; as the song develops these
    "men" reveal their dresses underneath. They play the re-
    mainder of the show in these dresses.*)

  MARVIN.
I NEED SLEEP.
I'M A GEM.
I'M AWAKE
AND IT'S THREE A.M.
DRINK SOME TEA, SEE IT'S FIVE
AND I'M STILL HERE ALIVE.
GOD, I'M SICK OF COUNTING ROWS OF SHEEP.
I CAN'T SLEEP.

STILL AWAKE.
  LADIES.
LA LA LA LA.
  MARVIN.
GIVE ME PEACE.
  LADIES.
LA. LA.
  MARVIN.
MAKE THEM CEASE—

LADIES.
MAKE THEM CEASE.
MARVIN.
—THEIR ABUSIVE CHATTER.
IT'S ROMANCE HE BEWARES,
AND PERCHANCE—
LADIES.
WELL, WHO CARES?
MARVIN.
SO I'M TURNING OUT THE BEDROOM LIGHT.
IT'S A FIGHT.
SHIT.
LADIES.
12 O'CLOCK.
MARVIN.
GOOD NIGHT.
LADIES.
1 O'CLOCK.
MARVIN.
I'M READING.
LADIES.
2 O'CLOCK.
MARVIN.
I'M STILL AWAKE AND THINKING.
LADIES.
WHAT?
MARVIN.
MAYBE I'LL BE . . .
LADIES. (*louder*)
WHAT?
MARVIN.
BECOME A . . .
LADIES. (*angry*)
WHAT?
MARVIN. (*softly, frightened they'll yell at him more*)
A NUN.
LADIES. (*loud*)
GO TO SLEEP.
MARVIN.
MAYBE NONE OF THE ABOVE.
MAYBE ONE DAY . . .
LADIES.
MAYBE ONE DAY . . .

MARVIN.
I'LL WIN.
LADIES.
WE LOVE YOU.
MARVIN.
AT LOVE.
WIFE.
I LOVE YOU.
MARVIN.
AT LOVE.   LADIES.
AT LOVE.   WE LOVE YOU.

I CAN'T TALK.
SWEETHEART.
HE CAN'T TALK.
MARVIN.
I GOT PHLEGM.
GOLDBERG.
HE'S GOT PHLEGM.
MARVIN.
'CAUSE OF THEM.
LADIES.
LA LA LA LA.
MARVIN.
THEY ABUSE MY REASON.
HOW THEY FI-RE MY PIQUE, (*pronounced: "peek"*)
'CAUSE MY BLADDER IS WEAK,
AND THEY NEVER REALLY DISAPPEAR
AND I'D LIKE SO MUCH TO WHIZZ
WITHOUT THEM THERE.

LADIES.
LOOK OUT, LOOK OUT, THE MAN'S A FOOL.
LOOK OUT, THE MAN'S APPEALING.
LOOK OUT, HE BREAKS THE GOLDEN RULE.
LOOK OUT, WHAT HE'S CONCEALING.

LOOK INTO MARVIN'S HEAD.
MARVIN.
WHO CAN REBUILD
THE PEOPLE I'VE KILLED
IN BED?

GOLDBERG.
OHHHHH . . .

MARVIN.
I NEED LIPS.
I NEED ARMS.
I NEED . . . WHAT?
LADIES.
WHAT?
MARVIN.
I NEED BOMBS EXPLODING.
IT'S IMPORTANT TO WIN
BUT I'M SCARED TO BEGIN.
SO I CHOOSE TO LOOK BEFORE I LEAP.
AND I LEAP.

I NEED—
LADIES.
SIX O'CLOCK
MARVIN.
SLEEP.
LADIES.
SIX-OH-FIVE.
MARVIN.
EXHAUSTED.
LADIES.
SIX FIFTEEN.
MARVIN.
I THINK PERHAPS I'M DREAMING OF . . .
LADIES.
MAYBE BREASTS.
MARVIN.
A CHEST.
LADIES.
AND LEGS.
MARVIN.
AND THIGHS . . .

MAYBE NONE OF THE ABOVE.
LADIES.
LET HIM SLEEP.
MARVIN.
AND DREAM.

LADIES.
AND DREAM.
MARVIN.
AND WIN . . .
LADIES.
WE LOVE YOU.
MARVIN.
AT LOVE.
SWEETHEART.
I LOVE YOU.
MARVIN.
AT LOVE.   LADIES.
AT LOVE.   WE LOVE YOU.

I'M ASLEEP.
WIFE.
CLOSE YOUR EYES.
MARVIN.
WILL IT KEEP?
LADIES.
IT WILL KEEP.
HE WILL PRIZE HIS SLUMBER.
MARVIN.
I COULD SLEEP THROUGH THE DAY
IF THEY'D JUST SLIP AWAY
LADIES.
BUT WE REAPPEAR WITH EVERY BREATH.
MARVIN.
I ACCEPT MY FAULTS
AND WELCOME SUDDEN DEATH.

LADIES.
LOOK OUT, LOOK OUT, THE MAN'S A FOOL.
LOOK OUT, THE MAN'S APPEALING.
LOOK OUT, HE BREAKS THE GOLDEN RULE.
LOOK OUT, WHAT HE'S CONCEALING.

ALL.
LOOK INTO MARVIN'S HEAD.
MARVIN.
WHO CAN REBUILD
THE PEOPLE I'VE KILLED
IN BED?

LADIES.
OHHH . . .
  ALL.
GIVE
HIM
SLEEP
AND . . .
  LADIES.
GIVE HIM SLEEP AND . . .
GIVE HIM SLEEP AND . . .
  ALL.
GIVE HIM SLEEP AND
LOVE!

A HELLUVA DAY (3)

(*where MARVIN sleeps and his wife tries to wake him*)

(*Alarm clocks rings.*)

WIFE.
IT'S A HELLUVA DAY.
IT'S A WONDERFUL MORNING.
WHAT A WONDERFUL WAY
TO SAY ALL'S FINE.
IT'S YOUR MOMENT TO SHINE.
JUST FORGET LAST NIGHT.
THIS ITTY-BITTY GLASS OF WINE
HELPS US START OUR DAY OUT RIGHT.
NOW COME AND EAT YOUR PETIT DEJEUNER.
TIME TO WAKE UP
TIME TO WAKE UP, MARVIN
AND FACE THE DAY.
LISTEN MY GRACE,
OUR EIGHT-YEAR-OLD IS CRYING
PLEASE SHOW YOUR FACE.

IT'S A NICE EASY HOUR
SOON I'M BELTING OUR CHILD
IN AN HOUR IT'S TIME TO CLIMB THE WALLS.
IF OUR EIGHT-YEAR-OLD CRAWLS
HOW SHOULD I REACT?
I THINK HE PLAYS WITH GIRLS AND DOLLS.
WHO CAN KNOW WHAT LOVE HE'S LACKED?
BUT ME, I TRY TO SEND
THOSE BLUES AWAY.
TIME TO WAKE UP
TIME TO WAKE UP, MARVIN
AND FACE THE DAY.
TIME TO WAKE UP
TIME TO . . .

MARVIN. What time is it?

(*The Venetian Blind is raised to reveal MISS GOLDBERG and
      SWEETHEART.*)

GOLDBERG.
TIME . . .
TO WAKE UP
TIME TO WAKE
 UP,
 MARVIN,
TIME TO WAKE
 UP,
 MARVIN,
TIME TO WAKE
 UP.

	WIFE.
TIME . . .	TIME TO WAKE
	UP,
	TIME TO WAKE
	UP,
TO WAKE UP,	MARVIN,
TIME TO WAKE	AND FACE THE
UP,	DAY . . .
MARVIN,	
TIME TO WAKE	
UP,	
MARVIN,	
TIME TO WAKE	
UP.	

		SWEETHEART.
(*quietly*)	(*quietly*)	(not *quietly*)
TIME . . .	TIME TO WAKE	WE . . .
	UP,	
	TIME TO WAKE	CAN'T STAND
	UP,	HERE,
TO WAKE UP,	MARVIN,	MARVIN,
TIME TO WAKE	AND FACE THE	WAITING FOR-
UP,	DAY.	EVER
MARVIN,		
TIME TO WAKE		SO, MOVE YOUR
UP.		ASS,
		MARVIN!

LADIES.
TIME TO WAKE UP
TIME TO WAKE UP, MARVIN . . .
AND FACE THE DAY.

I HAVE A FAMILY (4)

(*MARVIN sits up in bed and explains.*)

MARVIN.
SOMETHING'S MISSING
IN MY LIFE.
I DON'T KNOW WHAT IT IS
(THOUGH I'VE SUSPICIONS)
I CANNOT ACT ON THEM BECAUSE . . .

I HAVE A FAMILY.
AND A FAMILY PET.
AND A FAMILY THAT WILL GET UPSET
WHEN IT LEARNS WHY I SHOW STRESS.

I HAVE A FAMILY
WITH A WIFE WHO'S PERFECT IN MANY WAYS,
AND A DAZZLING SON
WHO WILL EARN HIS DAD STRAIGHT A's.

STILL I CAN SMELL THERE'S TROUBLE BREWING.
HOW CAN I TELL THAT SOMETHING'S DOING?
SOMETHING'S MISSING
IN MY MIND I'M KISSING
MEN . . .
NO. NO. NO. NO. START AGAIN.

(*a big smile*)
I HAVE A FAMILY.
WHICH I'VE NEVER DEFILED.
BUT I'M HONEST WHEN I SAY I'M A CHILD
FOR A FELLA'S CARESS.

PARDON ME WHILE I REGRESS.

HOW MARVIN EATS HIS BREAKFAST (5)

(MARVIN regresses to himself at an earlier age.)

LADIES. (*dressed as maids*)
How Marvin eats his breakfast.
How Marvin eats his breakfast.
How Marvin eats his breakfast.

MARVIN.
I LOVE BEING MARVIN!
I LOVE BEING MARVIN!
MARVIN TURNED FOURTEEN TODAY
AND EATS THE VERY BEST BREAKFAST IN TOWN.

LADIES.
How Marvin eats his breakfast.

MARVIN.
EVERYBODY INTO THE KITCHEN.
HERE COMES
MARVIN.
BANGING HIS GROIN WITH HIS FIST.
LADIES.
HE MUMBLES IN,
TO INSIST:
MARVIN.
NO ONE LOOKS BUSY IN THIS KITCHEN
AND MY BREAKFAST ISN'T READY
AND MY STOMACH ACHES.
I MEAN SPECIFICALLY THE MAID
WHO IS RECLINING LIKE SHE LAID THE GOLDEN EGG.
I WANT SOME CHATTER AND SOME GRUEL
MAKE ME WANT TO DROOL
TRY TO MAKE ME HUNGRY.
LADIES.
OHHH . . .
MARVIN.
CAT GOT YOUR TONGUE?
LADIES.
MARVIN ALWAYS KNOWS THE SORT OF ANSWERS
  HE'LL ALLOW.

MARVIN.
I MAY BE SLY DEAR, BUT NOT YOUNG.
  LADIES.
"WAIT UNTIL I'M OLDER THEN I'LL KILL YOU"
IS HIS ONE UNSPOKEN VOW.
  MARVIN.
I NEED MY BREAKFAST *NOW*!

(*Drum break.*)

  ALL.
EVERYBODY INTO THE KITCHEN
HERE COMES
MARVIN.
  LADIES.
AIMING A GUN AT THE MAID:
HE SHOOTS HER HEAD, SHE FALLS DEAD.
  MARVIN.
OH JESUS CHRIST IT WASN'T LOADED
SHE'S AN ACTRESS FROM THE OLD SCHOOL
AND A LOUSY CHEF.
I DON'T WANT MIRACLES FROM HEAVEN
JUST SOME EGGIES OVER SPINACH OVER TOAST.

NO, I WILL NOT APOLOGIZE!
SHE SHOULD WIN A PRIZE:
"VERY BEST
EMOTING."
  LADIES.
OHHHH . . .
  MARVIN.
THAT GIRL CAN'T COOK.
  LADIES.
MAYBE SHE CAN'T COOK
BUT HAVE YOU SEEN HER MILK A COW?
  MARVIN.
AND I CAN READ HER LIKE A BOOK.
  LADIES.
MARVIN WOULDN'T READ THAT KIND OF NOVEL
  ANYHOW.
  MARVIN.
I NEED MY BREAKFAST
NOW!

(*Drum break.*)

MARVIN.
PEOPLE, PEOPLE
LADIES.
PEOPLE, PEOPLE
MARVIN.
STOP YOUR STARING
LADIES.
STOP YOUR STARING
MARVIN.
PEOPLE, PEOPLE
STOP YOUR STARING
GET TO WORK
MY BREAKFAST ISN'T MADE YET.
LADIES.
PEOPLE, PEOPLE
STOP YOUR STARING
GET TO WORK
HIS BREAKFAST ISN'T . . .
ALL.
LIFE IS LONELY.
LIFE IS ROTTEN.
MARVIN.
AND THANKFULLY SHORT,
THANKFULLY SHORT,
THANKFULLY SHORT.
LADIES. (*spoken*) Like Marvin.
MARVIN.
EVERYBODY INTO THE KITCHEN.
HERE COMES
(*like an engine*) M-M-M-M-M-M-M- . . .
LADIES.
MARVIN!
MARVIN.
MARVIN!
LADIES.
WAVING HIS HANDS LIKE A TWIT.
HE THROWS A FIT,
THEN A KNIFE.
MARVIN.
YOU CALL THIS BREAKFAST ON MY BIRTHDAY?
THIS IS SHIT, THIS ISN'T BREAKFAST

I COULD CRACK YOUR FEET.
   LADIES.
NO, NO . . .
   MARVIN.
I MEAN FOR GOD'S SAKE
AM I TALKING TO THE WALL?
WHEN I SAY BREAKFAST
I MEAN FOOD.

I DREAMT ALL NIGHT OF HIPS AND LEGS
NOW I WANT SOME EGGS
THINGS I MIGHT
RELATE TO.
   LADIES.
OHHHH . . .
   MARVIN.
I'M JUST A SPRITE.
   LADIES.
MARVIN UNDERESTIMATES THE FEAR THAT HE'LL
  ENDOW.
   MARVIN.
I'LL WAIT HERE 'TIL YOU GET IT RIGHT!
   LADIES.
DO I?
DO I REALLY?
DO I REALLY HAVE TO SHOW YOU PEOPLE HOW?
   MARVIN.
I . . .
   ALL.
NEED MY BREAKFAST
NOW!

MARVIN'S GIDDY SEIZURES (6)

(The regression continues . . .)

SWEETHEART. Marvin?
MARVIN IS A BOY WHO HAS GIDDY SEIZURES
HE'S LAUGHING ALL THE TIME.
MARVIN IS A BOY WHO HAS GIDDY SEIZURES
SOMETIMES THEY'RE FATAL.
WHEN HE TURNS UPSIDE DOWN LIKE A LADLE
  POURING SOUP
HE'S A VERITABLE FOOL.
MARVIN IS MY VERY BEST FRIEND IN SCHOOL
IT'S ME
AND MARVIN.

LATELY I'VE BEEN THINKING MAYBE MARVIN NEEDS
  ATTENTION
OF A PRIVATE SORT.
MAYBE THIS WHOLE SEIZURE THING
IS SOMETHING HE INVENTED;
OR IS IT MEDICINAL?
  WIFE.
SHOULD HIS MOTHER BE BLAMED?
  SWEETHEART.
NO!
MARVIN HAS A SOMETHING WHICH MOST EVERY-
  BODY NEEDS
HE CANNOT EVER BE EMBARRASSED.
MARVIN IS MY VERY BEST FRIEND IN SCHOOL.
  WIFE.
AND SHE'S EMBARRASSED AND ASHAMED.
  MARVIN.
OH
  LADIES.
NO, NO.
  MARVIN.
OH
  LADIES.
NO, NO.

MARVIN'S GIDDY SEIZURES
MARVIN NEEDS LOVE
HE NEEDS LOVE,
HE NEEDS LOVE,
HE NEEDS LOVE.
OOOOOO . . .

MY HIGH SCHOOL SWEETHEART (7)

(*. . . and continues.*)

SWEETHEART.
MY HIGH SCHOOL SWEETHEART IS A PERSON, TOO.
I TELL HIM HE'S A PERSON.
HE SAYS I'M JUST RIDICKALOUS.
MY HIGH SCHOOL SWEETHEART
IS A TOO RIDICKALOUS SWEETHEART
WHO'S A—
  WIFE AND GOLDBERG.
—WHO'S A—
  SWEETHEART.
—PERSON TOO.
HE'S A PERSON.

I WANT TO HOLD HIM BUT HE'S NOT ALIVE
REPEAT THAT I'M A PERSON.
HE SAYS I'M JUST RIDICKALOUS.
MY HIGH SCHOOL SWEETHEART
IS A TOO RIDICKALOUS SWEETHEART
WHO'S A—
  ALL.
—WHO'S A—
  SWEETHEART.
—PERSON TOO.
HE'S A PERSON.

I SAY A PERSON HAS HER WANTS AND NEEDS.
I'M NOT A GREEDY PERSON.
HE SAYS I'M JUST *RIDICKALOUS*!
I'M JUST RIDICKALOUS,
I'M A TOO RIDICKALOUS SWEETHEART
WHO'S A—
  ALL.
—WHO'S A—
  SWEETHEART.
—PERSON TOO.
  ALL.
WE'RE A PERSON

GOLDBERG.
HE'S A PERSON.

HE'S A PERSON.
MARVIN.
I'M A PERSON.

I'M A PERSON.
SWEETHEART.
I'M A PERSON.

I'M A PERSON.

I'M A PERSON.
LADIES.
I'M A PERSON

SWEETHEART.
I'M A PERSON.

I'M A PERSON.
WIFE.
HE'S A PERSON.
WIFE & GOLDBERG.
HE'S A PERSON.
MARVIN.
HE'S A PERSON.
WIFE & GOLDBERG.
HE'S A PERSON.
MARVIN.
I'M A PERSON.

I'M A PERSON.

SWEETHEART.
HERE I AM, MARVIN, HOLD ME
I WANT YOU
TO WANT ME BADLY
LOVE ME MADLY
PUT ME ONTO YOUR BED;
NOT A PED-
ESTAL.
WILL YOU?
PLEASE DO.
ALL.
MARVIN LOVES MISS GOLDBERG.
SWEETHEART.
BUT, I'M HIS SWEETHEART.
MARVIN.
I LOVE MISS GOLDBERG.
SHE CAST ME IN HER PLAY
SHE GAVE ME WORDS TO SAY
MADE ME WHAT I AM TODAY
SWEETHEART.
I'M HIS SWEETHEART.
MARVIN.
I AM COLUMBUS.
WIFE.
I'M A PERSON.

MARVIN.
COLUMBUS.
SWEETHEART.
I'M HIS SWEETHEART.
MARVIN.
KING OF THE OCEAN.
WIFE AND SWEETHEART.
I'M A PERSON . . .
MARVIN.
COLUMBUS . . .

Christopher Columbus as you recall had three ships: the Nina, the Pinta, and the Santa Maria, the Santa Maria being the best looking of the three, lots of gold and carved wood. Even the Pinta had its admirers. But it was the Nina that Christopher was fondest of—'cause it was named after his mother, Nina Columbus.

GOLDBERG.
GO AHEAD.
PLAY COLUMBUS.
STOP MAKING ME CRAZY, MARVIN
CRAZY MARVIN
I LOVE THE WAY MARVIN ACTS
I DO.
DO NOT MAKE FACES
AND DO NOT UNDO THE FACTS
RELAX. RELAX. RELAX. RELAX.
ALL.
RELAX. RELAX. RELAX. RELAX.

GOLDBERG & MARVIN.	WIFE & SWEETHEART.
GO AHEAD.	RELAX.
PLAY COLUMBUS.	RELAX.
STOP MAKING ME CRAZY, MARVIN,	RELAX.
CRAZY MARVIN	RELAX. RELAX.
I LOVE THE WAY MARVIN ACTS	RELAX. RELAX.
I DO.	RELAX. RELAX.
DO NOT MAKE FACES	RELAX. RELAX.
AND DO NOT UNDO THE FACTS	RELAX. RELAX.

ALL.
RELAX. RELAX. RELAX. RELAX.

GOLDBERG. Queen Isabella—this is not often told to 9th graders—but here goes:

MARVIN. Queen Isabella, who financed Columbus' trip to America, was his secret girlfriend.

WIFE & SWEETHEART.

A historical fact.

MARVIN. He was her date at a cotillion given by Spanish high society on the occasion of her inauguration; but because he wasn't royalty, he was made to sit upstairs in her bedroom and, while she cavorted downstairs, he read back issues of *Stella d'oro* and other 15th century periodicals.

GOLDBERG. (*or* MARVIN) Columbus later said:

MARVIN. It was one of the best nights of my life.

LADIES.

HE LOVES MISS GOLDBERG.

MARVIN.

SHE CAST ME IN HER PLAY.

SHE GAVE ME WORDS TO SAY.

MADE ME WHAT I AM TODAY.

SWEETHEART.

I'M HIS SWEETHEART.

MARVIN.

I AM COLUMBUS . . .

WIFE.

I'M A PERSON.

MARVIN.

. . . COLUMBUS . . .

SWEETHEART.	WIFE & GOLDBERG.
I'M HIS SWEETHEART.	I'M A PERSON.

MARVIN.

. . . KING OF THE OCEAN . . .

SWEETHEART.	WIFE & GOLDBERG.
I'M HIS SWEETHEART.	I'M A PERSON.

MARVIN.

. . . COLUMBUS!

Columbus' last words were: "I only wish I could have discovered Europe."

GOLDBERG. Oh, Marvin!

SET THOSE SAILS (8)

(MARVIN's teacher gets ridiculously excited
by the Columbus story. Her exhortation:)

GOLDBERG.
THE WORLD IS ROUND.
THERE'S A KEY TO EVERY DOOR.
THAT'S WHAT OUR HERO FOUND.
NOTHING IS FOR NOTHING
AND A NEW LAND IS A NEW LAND TO EXPLORE.
NOT JUST PATHS YOU RETRACE.
I'M TALKING MOUNTAINS AND SPACE.

HEY, I LOVE YOU
SET THOSE SAILS.
A GOOD MAN NEVER
   FAILS.

HEY, I LOVE YOU
SET THOSE SAILS.
A GOOD MAN NEVER
   FAILS.

LADIES.
HEY, I LOVE YOU
SET THOSE SAILS.
A GOOD MAN NEVER
   FAILS.

HEY, I LOVE YOU
SET THOSE SAILS.
A GOOD MAN NEVER
   FAILS.

WATCH ME CLOSE.
CLOSE YOUR EYES.
I AM LIVING PROOF THAT COWARDS
STILL CAN RISE.
YOU MIGHT TELL ME YOU'RE A VICTIM,
YOU MIGHT GET WHAT YOU DESERVE.
BUT, I WON'T EXCUSE,
   LADIES.
BOY, I CAN'T EXCUSE
   GOLDBERG.
A BOY WHO'S LOST HIS NERVE.

O LORD SET SAIL.
BE PREPARING FOR A FALL.
STAY CLEAR OF LOVE AND JAIL.

LOVERS DON'T GO HUNGRY
AND THE APPETITE OF YOUNG MEN COUNTS FOR ALL.
LORD, IT'S ROUGH IN THE SACK,
KIDS LIVE AND LEARN TO ATTACK.

WIFE & SWEETHEART.
HEY, I LOVE YOU
SET THOSE SAILS.
A GOOD MAN NEVER
   FAILS.

GOLDBERG.
HEY, I LOVE YOU
SET THOSE SAILS.
A GOOD MAN NEVER
   FAILS.

HEY, I LOVE YOU
SET THOSE SAILS.
A GOOD MAN NEVER
   FAILS.

HEY, I LOVE YOU
SET THOSE SAILS.
A GOOD MAN NEVER
   FAILS.

HEY, I LOVE YOU
SET THOSE SAILS.
A GOOD MAN NEVER
   FAILS.
HEY, I LOVE YOU
SET THOSE SAILS.
A GOOD MAN NEVER FAILS.

(*GOLDBERG continues to
riff gospel style.*)

HEY, I LOVE YOU
SET THOSE SAILS.
A GOOD MAN NEVER . . .
   GOLDBERG.
A GOOD MAN NEVER
FAILS . . .

A GOOD MAN NEVER . . .
   ALL THREE.
FAILS.

I SWEAR I WON'T EVER AGAIN (Part 1) (9)

(MARVIN is back in the present, whining.)

LADIES.
RELAX. RELAX. RELAX. RELAX.

SWEETHEART. Relax, Marvin.

MARVIN.
MY WIFE, MY WIFE
IT'S ALL SO CLEAR:
SHE'S SWEET
AND DEARLY NEEDS ME.
SHE NEEDS MY LIFE
(MY WIFE)
AND I'D GIVE IT IF I COULD;
THAT'S SO FREQUENTLY THE MOST MISUNDERSTOOD.
LAZILY I LOVE HER.
CRAZILY I HATE HER.
OFTEN I DEBATE HER
EVERY OTHER NIGHT.

I'M IN THE RIGHT,
SHE'S IN THE RIGHT.
I'M IN THE WRONG,
SHE'S IN THE RIGHT, DAMMIT.
WE GET ALONG,
BUT ALWAYS FIGHT, DAMMIT.
SHE ALWAYS WINS, BUT ALWAYS CRIES;
AND IT'S ME AND THEM
(ME AND MEN)
ME AND WHOMEVER
I SWEAR I WON'T EVER AGAIN.

MY KID, MY SON,
HE NEEDS A PLAN.
IN SHORT,
A MAN TO LEAD HIM.
I'LL MAKE IT FUN—
MY ONLY SON—
DADDY HEARS HIS BOYCHICK TALK

DADDY WANTS TO BE THE BEST GUY ON THE BLOCK.
MOMMY SAYS YOU'RE FUNNY.
SHOW ME HOW YOU'RE FUNNY.
DADDY MAKES GOOD MONEY.
THAT'S WHAT DADDY'S FOR.

HIM I ADORE,
ME HE'LL DESPISE.
I ASK FOR MORE
HE'D CROSS HIS EYES AT ME.
LET US EXPLORE
HE'D COMPROMISE THAT WE
LIE ON THE FLOOR AND FANTASIZE . . .

HIGH SCHOOL LADIES AT FIVE O'CLOCK (10)

(*a calypso fantasy*)

SWEETHEART.
YOO HOO!
  WIFE.
  YOO HOO!
    GOLDBERG.
    YOO HOO!
SWEETHEART.
YOO HOO!
  WIFE.
  YOO HOO!
    GOLDBERG.
    YOO HOO!

SWEETHEART.
HIGH SCHOOL LADIES AT FIVE O'CLOCK
WE BE GOOD GIRLS ALL,
PRACTICING ADVENTURES
OF A SORT WHICH DIVERT YOU
BUT WHICH NEVER EVER TRY TO HURT YOU.
HIGH SCHOOL LADIES AT FIVE O'CLOCK

  LADIES.
WE SING LA LA LA LA
LA LA LA
WE SING LA LA LA LA
  SWEETHEART.
OH HOW THEY REPITITIOUS.
  LADIES.
LA LA LA LA
MUMBLE AND WALK
YOU SEE THEM?
HIGH SCHOOL LADIES AT FIVE O'CLOCK,
NOW,

  SWEETHEART.
MARVIN, TAKE A BREAK
MARVIN, I'M YOUR SWEETIE
MARVIN, DANCE, BOY, DANCE

WE ARE YOUR IMAGINATION.
BUY YOURSELF A MALTED
AND WE'LL DRINK IT AND TALK
BUT COME TO HIGH SCHOOL LADIES AT FIVE
  O'CLOCK.

  LADIES.
THEY SING LA LA LA LA
LA LA LA
THEY SING LA LA LA LA
  SWEETHEART.
OH HOW THEY REPITITIOUS.
  LADIES.
LA LA LA LA
MUMBLE AND WALK
HIGH SCHOOL LADIES AT FIVE O'CLOCK,
NOW,
  SWEETHEART.
LA LA LA LA
LA LA LA LA
LA LA LA LA
LA LA LA LA
LA LA LA LA
LA LA LEY . . . HEY!

WIFE & GOLDBERG.	SWEETHEART.
LA LA LA LA	LA LA
LA LA LA	LA LA LA LA
THEY SING LA LA LA LA	LA LA LA LA
	LA LA LA LA
	LA LA LA LA
LA LA LA LA	LA LA LA LA
MUMBLE AND WALK	LA LA LEY . . .
HIGH SCHOOL LADIES	
AT FIVE O'CLOCK, NOW	HEY
SWEETHEART.	
HIGH SCHOOL . . .	WIFE & GOLDBERG.
	HIGH SCHOOL!
LADIES AT FIVE O'CLOCK.	
HIGH SCHOOL . . .	
	HIGH SCHOOL!
LADIES AT FIVE O'CLOCK.	
HIGH SCHOOL . . .	

HIGH SCHOOL!

LADIES AT FIVE O'CLOCK.
  WIFE.
HOICHY CHOMBO.
  GOLDBERG.
HOICHY CHOMBO.
  SWEETHEART.
HOICHY CHOMBO.
HIGH SCHOOL . . .   WIFE & GOLDBERG.
                            HIGH SCHOOL!

LADIES AT FIVE O'CLOCK.
HIGH SCHOOL . . .

                            HIGH SCHOOL!

LADIES AT FIVE O'CLOCK.
HIGH SCHOOL . . .

                            HIGH SCHOOL!

LADIES AT FIVE . . .
  WIFE.
NOT ONE.
  GOLDBERG.
NOT TWO.
  SWEETHEART.
NOT THREE
  WIFE & GOLDBERG.
NOT FOUR
  LADIES.
BUT FIVE O'CLOCK . . .
(*seductively*) OOOO!
  SWEETHEART.
DOES HE LIKE THE RAIN?
  GOLDBERG & WIFE.
OH YES HE DO!
  SWEETHEART.
IS HE BETTER THAN BANANA?
  MARVIN.
AAAAHHH!
  SWEETHEART.
DOES HE LIKE THE SNOW?
  GOLDBERG & WIFE.
OH YES HE DO!
  SWEETHEART.
IS HE BETTER THAN BANANA?

MARVIN.
AAAAHHH!
  SWEETHEART.
DOES HE KISS?
  LADIES.
NO.
  SWEETHEART.
TOUCH?
  LADIES.
NO.
  SWEETHEART.
DRINK?
  LADIES.
NO.
  SWEETHEART.
SCREW?
  LADIES.
NO!

  ALL.
HIGH SCHOOL LADIES AT NINE A.M.
WE BE WAITING AT THE SCHOOL.
WE ADMIRIN' THE PHOTOGRAPH
OF MARVIN ON THE STAGE
TURN THE PAGE
AND LOOK AT
HIGH SCHOOL LADIES AT FIVE O'CLOCK.

  SWEETHEART.
DOES HE LIKE?

DOES HE LIKE TO SCREW?
DOES HE LIKE?

DOES HE LIKE TO SCREW?
DOES HE LIKE?

DOES HE LIKE TO SCREW
HIS FRIENDS?

DOES HE?
  LADIES.
DOES HE?

  WIFE & GOLDBERG.
DOES HE LIKE?

DOES HE LIKE?

DOES HE LIKE?

Marvin.
DOES HE?
  Sweetheart.
DOES HE LIKE?   Wife & Goldberg.

                                 DOES HE LIKE?
DOES HE LIKE TO SCREW?
DOES HE LIKE?

                                 DOES HE LIKE?
DOES HE LIKE TO SCREW?
DOES HE LIKE?

                                 DOES HE LIKE?
DOES HE LIKE TO SCREW
HIS . . .
DOES HE?
  Wife.
DOES HE?
  Sweetheart.
DOES HE?
  Goldberg.
DOES HE?
  Sweetheart.
DOES HE?
  Wife.
DOES HE?
  Sweetheart.
DOES HE?
  Goldberg.
DOES HE?
  Sweetheart.
DOES HE?
  Wife.
DOES HE?
  Sweetheart.
DOES HE?
  Goldberg.
DOES HE?
  Sweetheart.
DOES HE?
  Wife.
DOES HE?
  Sweetheart.
DOES HE?
  Goldberg.
DOES HE?

I SWEAR I WON'T EVER AGAIN (Part 2) (11)

MARVIN.
THEM I ADORED.
ME THEY DESPISED.
I ASKED FOR MORE
THEY'D CROSS THEIR EYES AT ME
LET US EXPLORE
THEY'D COMPROMISE THAT WE
LIE ON THE FLOOR AND FANTASIZE . . .

THE RAPE OF MISS GOLDBERG by Marvin (12)

(*a fantasy which is better abstracted*)

SWEETHEART. "The Rape of Miss Goldberg"—by Marvin.
Scene One.

MARVIN.
HI MISS GOLDBERG AT YOUR DESK.
MY NAME'S MARVIN WE'RE ALONE AT LAST.
I TURNED FOURTEEN JUST TODAY
AND I THOUGHT FOR A NOT UNSEEMLY PRICE,
YOU'D INTRODUCE ME TO THE WONDERS OF THE BED
AND ALSO TREAT ME NICE.

I'M THE BOY WHO THROWS THE FITS.
HE WHO PUTS THE CHALK INSIDE HIS EAR.
DO YOU KNOW ME FROM A HOLE IN THE WALL?
MARVIN'S CUTE THOUGH RARELY GOOD.
BUT, DEAREST, PLEASE ACCEPT MY HAND
MISS GOLDBERG WHO
IS PERFECT WOMANHOOD.

SWEETHEART. Scene Two.

GOLDBERG.
MARVIN HOW,
TELL ME HOW DID YOU GET IN HERE PLEASE?
MARVIN.
I DRUGGED THE MAN WHO WAS GUARDING THE
FLOOR.
GOLDBERG.
MARVIN OPEN UP THE DOOR.
MARVIN PLEASE TURN ON THE LIGHT.
MARVIN LISTEN,
I'M THE ONLY ONE HERE IN THE SCHOOL
EXCEPT YOU,
AND THE GUARD WHO YOU BEAT IN A FIGHT.
MARVIN.
HE WAS DRUGGED.
GOLDBERG.
HE WAS DRUGGED.

MARVIN.
NOT WITH PILLS.
GOLDBERG.
THEN WITH WHAT?
MARVIN.
WITH SOME APPLES FROM A BASKET.
WOULD YOU LIKE A FEW MISS GOLDBERG?
WHAT I DO FOR YOU MISS GOLDBERG
IS YOUR PLEASURE.

SWEETHEART. Scene Three.

GOLDBERG.
WHY SHOULD MARVIN JUMP ON MISS GOLDBERG?
WHY DOES MARVIN DUMP ON MISS GOLDBERG?
I KNEW,
WHEN I FIRST LOOKED INTO HIS EYES.
MARVIN.
I LIKE YOUR EYES MISS GOLDBERG.
GOLDBERG.
LIES!
HE HAS NEVER SEEN MY FACE.
MARVIN.
I HAVE NEVER SEEN YOUR EYES.
GOLDBERG.
I WAS NEVER OUT OF PLACE.
I TAUGHT.
MARVIN.
THAT'S TRUE.
SHE MINDED HER BUSINESS.
SHE TAUGHT . . .
GOLDBERG.
. . . I TAUGHT AND I MINDED MY BUSINESS.
MARVIN.
BUT THE BUSINESS AT HAND . . .
GOLDBERG.
KEEP YOUR HANDS OFF MY EYES!
MARVIN.
BUT THE BUSINESS AT HAND . . .
GOLDBERG.
KEEP YOUR HANDS OFF MY EYES!

MARVIN.
BUT THE BUSINESS AT HAND
IS . . .

SWEETHEART. Scene Four.

MARVIN.
I ALWAYS LIKED THE WAY YOU WORE YOUR GLASSES.
IN AND OUT OF CLASSES.
I ALWAYS LIKED THE WAY YOU GOT ANGRY IN
    YOUR GLASSES.
THAT'S COOL
MISS GOLDBERG.
I ALWAYS THOUGHT THOSE GLASSES HID YOUR
    PASSION.
THAT'S MISS GOLDBERG'S FASHION, I SAID.
NOW IT'S MY BIRTHDAY AND HERE'S MY SURPRISE:
I'M GONNA SEE YOUR EYES MISS GOLDBERG.
I'M GONNA SEE YOUR EYES MY DARLING!
    GOLDBERG.
DON'T TOUCH MY GODDAMN EYES,
YOU LITTLE SHIT,
I'LL THROW A FIT.
I'LL BEAT YOUR HEAD IN WITH A HAMMER!

SWEETHEART. (laughs) Scene Five.

GOLDBERG.
MY EYES ARE MY EYES.
YOUR HANDS ARE YOUR HANDS.
JUST KEEP YOUR DIRTY FINGERS AWAY FROM MY
    FACE KID.
THAT'S THE ONLY THING MISS GOLDBERG DEMANDS.

MARVIN. Now move.

SWEETHEART. Scene six.

MARVIN. Now move! *Now Move!*
LISTEN I'M A BASTARD
BUMMER WITH A PENIS

AND I MEAN US TWO TO BE TOGETHER
TEACHER, YES I DO, I DO
I MEAN US TWO TO SCREW TOGETHER
ME TOGETHER
YOU TOGETHER
MISS GOLDBERG?

   GOLDBERG.
WHAT?

   MARVIN.
MISS GOLDBERG?

   GOLDBERG.
WHAT?

   MARVIN.
MAKE MARVIN A HAPPY BOY!
(*MISS GOLDBERG screams.*)

   SWEETHEART. Scene Seven! One, two, three, four!

   MARVIN.
MISS GOLDBERG,
MISS GOLDBERG,
MISS GOLDBERG,
MISS GOLDBERG,
PLEASE, PLEASE, PLEASE,
RUB YOUR HANDS BETWEEN
YOUR HANDS BETWEEN   GOLDBERG.
  MY KNEES . . .

LA, LA, LA, LA	WHAT DOES MARVIN
LA, LA, LA, LA	WANT FROM MISS GOLD-BERG?
LA, LA, LA, LA	WHAT DOES MARVIN
LA, LA, LA, LA	WANT FROM MISS GOLD-BERG?
MISS GOLDBERG, MISS GOLDBERG	WHAT DOES MARVIN
MISS GOLDBERG, MISS GOLDBERG	WANT FROM MISS GOLD-BERG?
PLEASE, PLEASE, PLEASE, PLEASE	WHAT DOES MARVIN
PLEASE, PLEASE, PLEASE PLEASE	WANT FROM MISS GOLD-BERG?
PLEASE, PLEASE, PLEASE, PLEASE	WHAT DOES MARVIN

PLEASE, PLEASE,   WANT FROM MISS GOLD-
    PLEASE, PLEASE   BERG?
PLEASE!!

Sweetheart. Scene Eight.

Marvin.
MARVIN ALWAYS GETS THE THINGS
HE WANTS.
    Goldberg.
EXCEPT THE THINGS
HE WANTS.
    Marvin.
HE GETS THE THINGS
HE WANTS.
    Goldberg.
MARVIN   Marvin.
ALWAYS GETS THE   MARVIN
    THINGS
HE WANTS   ALWAYS
EXCEPT THE   GETS THE
THINGS HE WANTS.   THINGS HE WANTS.
    Marvin.
HE GETS THE THINGS . . .
    Goldberg.
EXCEPT THE THINGS . . .
    Marvin.
HE GETS THE THINGS . . .
    Goldberg.
EXCEPT THE THINGS . . .
    Marvin & Goldberg.
HE . . .
    Sweetheart.
WANTS . . .

Marvin. Do you want my telephone number?
Sweetheart. Curtain!

I SWEAR I WON'T EVER AGAIN (Part 3) (13)

(in the present once again)

MARVIN.
I'M IN THE RIGHT,
SHE'S IN THE RIGHT.
I'M IN THE WRONG,
SHE'S IN THE RIGHT, DAMMIT.
WE GET ALONG
BUT ALWAYS FIGHT, DAMMIT.
SHE ALWAYS WINS, BUT ALWAYS CRIES;
AND IT'S ME AND THEM
(ME AND MEN)
HELP ME TO SEVER
I SWEAR I WON'T EVER AGAIN.

YOU BE MY WITNESS.
ATTEST TO MY FITNESS
AS HUSBAND, AND FATHER, AND FRIEND.   LADIES.
DO NOT LET ME LOOK ASKANCE   OOOHHH . . .
KEEP A VIGIL NIGHTLY.
DISABUSE ME OF ROMANCE
MAKE ME SEEM UNSIGHTLY.
I CAN'T KNOW THE OUTCOME.

BUT, I'LL TRY.   OOOHHH . . .
I'LL TRY.   AHHHHH . . .
I'LL TRY.

I LOVE MY WIFE.
SHE LOVES HER BOYS.
SHE LOVES THE NOISE OF FAMILY LIVING.
I LOVE THE JOYS OF NEVER FORGIVING.
NO ONE DESTROYS THE FAMILY
  LADIES.
NO ONE DESTROYS THE FAMILY
  ALL.
NO ONE DESTROYS THE FAMILY
  MARVIN.
LEAST NOT ME AND THEM
ME AND MEN

GOD I'M SO CLEVER
I SWEAR I WON'T EVER AGAIN.
ME AND THEM.
ME AND MEN.
  ALL.
NEVER MEANS NEVER,
I SWEAR I WON'T EVER AGAIN . . .
  MARVIN.
AGAIN, AGAIN
NO MEN,
AGAIN.
  LADIES.
AHHH . . . DAT!

(*Blackout*)

LOVE ME FOR WHAT I AM (14)

(*A tiny patch of light opens on MARVIN's face . . . He forgot
    to say something.*)

MARVIN.
LEST I FORGET
SHE WILL ALWAYS REMIND ME
OF HOW WE TWO MET . . .

(*His wife talks about the time she met her husband.*)

WIFE.
I MET A MAN
IN THE CAN
WOULDN'T YOU KNOW HE WAS GOING MY WAY?
WE TALKED TILL FOUR
HE TALKED MORE.
I WAS AFRAID I'D TURN AND SAY:

"LOVE ME FOR WHAT I AM
NOT WHAT I TRY TO BE.
LOVE ME FOR WHAT I AM
I AM
SOMEONE IMPERFECTLY ME."

THE LIGHTS WERE LOW
DON'T YOU KNOW
HE GAVE ME A PHONY HOME ADDRESS.
GOLDBERG & SWEETHEART.
OH . . .
WIFE.
THEN AFTER WEEKS
GUESS WHO SPEAKS:
"DARLING" HE SAYS AND I SAY "YES"

"LOVE ME FOR WHAT I AM
NOT WHAT I TRY TO BE.
LOVE ME FOR WHAT I AM
I AM
A PERSON WHO LIKES TO LIE TOO MUCH
I TRY TOO MUCH

TO IMPRESS OTHER PEOPLE . . .
OFTEN MY INFERIORS."
    GOLDBERG & SWEETHEART.
OOOOO . . .

WIFE.	GOLDBERG & SWEETHEART.	MARVIN.
COULD YOU LIKE	LOVE, LOVE,	
A GIRL LIKE THAT?	LOVE, LOVE.	
COULD YOU LIKE	LOVE, LOVE,	
A GIRL LIKE THAT?	LOVE, LOVE.	MARVIN.
WOULD YOU HOLD	LOVE, LOVE.	A PERSON WHO LIKES
HER IN YOUR ARMS?	LOVE, LOVE,	TO LIE TOO MUCH.
COULD YOU LIKE	LOVE, LOVE.	I TRY TOO MUCH
A GIRL LIKE THAT?	LOVE, LOVE,	TO IMPRESS
COULD YOU LIKE	LOVE, LOVE.	OTHER PEO-PLE . . .
A GIRL LIKE THAT?	LOVE, LOVE,	OFTEN
COULD YOU LIKE	LOVE, LOVE.	MY INFERIORS.
A GIRL LIKE THAT?		

WIFE.
WE LAY IN BED.
HE PLAYS DEAD.
I PLAY A RECENT 45.
HE TURNS IT LOW
TALKS SO SLOW
"DARLING," HE SAYS
"WE MIGHT SURVIVE."

    GOLDBERG & SWEETHEART.
OOOO . . .

    WIFE & MARVIN.
LOVE ME FOR WHAT I AM
NOT WHAT I TRY TO BE.
LOVE ME FOR WHAT I AM
I AM
    WIFE.
SOMEONE IMPERFECTLY ME. . .
    MARVIN.
A PERSON WHO LIKES TO
LIE TOO MUCH
I TRY TOO MUCH . . .

    GOLDBERG & SWEETHEART.
LOVE, LOVE, LOVE
LOVE, LOVE, LOVE

Sweetheart.
SOMEONE IMPERFECTLY . . .
ME.
  Marvin.
ME.
  Wife and Marvin.
ME . . .
ME.

I AM WEARING A HAT (15)

(*at the wedding of MARVIN to his wife*)

GOLDBERG. (*to SWEETHEART*)
WATCH MARVIN AS HE TAKES HIS BRIDE.
THIS WHOLE DAMN THING'S A JOKE.
BEFORE THE ACT IS SANCTIFIED
PERHAPS HE'LL TRIP OR SHE MIGHT CHOKE.
FORGET THIS GUY HE'S NO DAMN GOOD . . .
NO ACTION AND ALL WORDS . . .
MARVIN IS SOMETIMES FOR THE BIRDS.

SWEETHEART. (*dressed in an enormous mourning hat*)
HIDE MY FACE.
CHANGE MY PLACE OF WORSHIP.
CALL ME A DISGRACE
AND THEN BE DONE WITH BLAME.
HOW WAS I TO KNOW
THAT HE'S A GIGOLO
EMOTIONALLY UNDERBRED?
WHEN THE PASSION STINGS
I THINK OF PRETTY THINGS
INSTEAD.

I AM WEARING A HAT.
AFTER WINTER, I'LL MARRY.
I'M ENTITLED TO THAT
I WEAR A HAT.
I WEAR A HAT.

HERE I SIT.
DRUNK AND SELF-INDULGENT.
DRESSED UP IN A HAT WHICH EVEN I DETEST.

SWEETHEART & GOLDBERG.
MARRY MONEY
MONEY WINS
YOUR PAST WILL DISAPPEAR
AND WITH IT ALL YOUR SINS.
JOY ONCE SEEMED SO NEAR,
NOW WHAT'S LEFT TO FEAR
BEGINS.

GOLDBERG.   SWEETHEART.
I AM WEARING
A HAT.   I AM WEARING
HE'D APPROVE   A HAT.
IF I LET HIM.   AFTER WINTER
SINCE THE WORLD'S   I'LL MARRY.
COME TO THAT.   I'M ENTITLED
I WEAR A HAT.   TO WEAR A HAT.

(*The WIFE marches on in her wedding gown.*)

GOLDBERG & SWEETHEART.
I REMEMBER MY PLACE.
THOUGH IT'S HARD TO FORGET HIM.
BUT HE CAN'T SEE MY FACE.
I WEAR A HAT.
I WEAR A HAT.

WIFE.
I WEAR A . . . HAT.
(*looks for MARVIN offstage*) Marvin?
LADIES.
HAT!

WEDDING SONG (16)

SWEETHEART & GOLDBERG.
WHERE'S HER GODDAMN HUSBAND?
WHERE'S THE GODDAMN AISLE?
ALWAYS ACTING INFANTILE.
THAT'S ONE THING THAT MAKES HIM SMILE.

(*MARVIN is pushed onstage.*)

MARVIN.
I DO NOT THINK THAT THIS WILL WORK.
I THINK WE SHOULD'VE SPOKE BEFORE.
BUT TODAY'S TOO LATE.
I HATE WEDDINGS.
SWEETHEART & GOLDBERG.
WE LOVE WEDDINGS.
SWEETHEART.
IS HER VEIL ON STRAIGHT?
GOLDBERG.
AND IS SHE DRUNK?
SWEETHEART.
I HOPE SO.
GOLDBERG.
DOES HE LOOK AT HER?
SWEETHEART. (*hopefully*)
OR LOOK AWAY?
GOLDBERG.
I DO NOT KNOW THE ANSWER.
WIFE.
WILL YOU BE THE MAN I'VE DREAMT ABOUT?
GOLDBERG & SWEETHEART.
ISN'T THIS A PERFECT DAY?

3 SECONDS (17)

MARVIN. (*deadpan*)
WHAT SHOULD I THINK ABOUT
FIVE SECONDS BEFORE I DIE?
WILL THE MAID UNPAID
STILL COME TUESDAY?
DID I PICK MY LAUNDRY UP
WEDNESDAY NIGHT?
AND THERE'S SOME MILK
ROTTING
IN MY REFRIGERATOR.
ROTTING AND STINKING UP THE OTHER FOOD
OF WHICH THERE ISN'T MUCH
BECAUSE I'M ABOUT TO DIE
AND I DIDN'T FEEL LIKE SHOPPING.
(*rimshot*)

WHAT DO I THINK ABOUT
FOUR SECONDS BEFORE I DIE?
DID I SAY GOODBYE
TO THE GIRLS FROM
　　HIGH SCHOOL?　　　　　　SWEETHEART & GOLDBERG.
　　　　　　　　　　　　　　BYE.

WHAT DO THEY WANT?
　　　　　　　　　　　　　　BYE. BYE.

IS THAT ENOUGH FOR
　　THEM?
　　　　　　　　　　　　　　BYE. BYE. BYE.

BYE.
　　　　　　　　　　　　　　BYE . . .

BYE.
　　　　　　　　　　　　　　BYE, BYE.
(*to SWEETHEART & GOLDBERG*)
PLEASE STOP YOUR BYE-ING.
HAVE PITY ON ONE WHO'S DYING.
FOUR SECONDS MY HEART WILL STOP.
FOUR SECONDS I CLOSE UP SHOP. HEY!
(*rimshot*)

WHAT DO I THINK ABOUT?
WHAT DO I THINK

WHAT DO I
WHAT DO I
WHAT DO I
WHAT DO I
WHAT DO I
WHAT DO I

WHAT DO I THINK ABOUT
THREE SECONDS BEFORE I DIE?
WHEN HER PASSION SOON COOLS,
AND IT WILL . . . IF SHE'S SMART.
WILL SHE COUNTENANCE FOOLS?
WILL I END WHAT I START?
WILL I BREAK A FEW RULES?
WILL I BREAK THE GIRL'S HEART?
DID I EVER HAVE . . .
NO. DID I EVER HAVE . . .
WILL I EVER HAVE FUN?
 LADIES.
THREE.
TWO.
ONE.

(*Machine gun fire. MARVIN screams. Silence. He opens his eyes. Feels his pulse. He walks dejectedly back to the wedding.*)

WEDDING SONG (Part 2) (18)

GOLDBERG. (*as the Rabbi*)
DO YOU TAKE
THIS WOMAN
TO BE YOUR WIFE?
   MARVIN.
I DO.
YES, I DO.
YES, I . . .
   GOLDBERG.
DO YOU TAKE THIS MAN TO BE YOUR HUSBAND?
   WIFE.
YES, I DOOOO.
YES, I DOOOOOO.
   MARVIN.
I DO TOO.

(*MARVIN stamps down to break the glass. He misses. Tries
   again. Misses. WIFE breaks the glass.*)

MARVIN. (*ruefully*) Mazel tov.

HOW THE BODY FALLS APART (18A)

(MARVIN is charmingly tearing apart WIFE's wedding gown during this song.)

LADIES.
HOW THE BODY FALLS APART
FIRST THE GROIN AND THEN THE HEART
IT'S EASY.
AND IT'S SMART.
THINGS ON WHICH WE MOST DEPEND
SEEM TO FAIL US IN THE END.
HOW LIKE
LIKE A BODY
WHEN THE BODY
FALLS
APART.

I FEEL HIM SLIPPING AWAY (19)

(*time passes*)

WIFE.
WE'VE BEEN MARRIED FOR TEN YEARS.
EIGHT WERE FINE; AND SIX WERE NOT.
IT SEEMED LONGER THAN TEN YEARS.
WHAT I RECALL IS BETTER FORGOT.

THE FIRST TWO WERE THE BEST YEARS:
WHEN THE KID WAS BORN,
WHEN THE WORLD SEEMED OKAY.

BUT I
I FELT HIM SLIPPING AWAY.
I FELT HIM DIE IN MY ARMS,
HIS CHARMS
WERE NOT FOR ME.
HOW COULD I EVER COMPETE?
THE CAUSE OF ALL HIS LUST—
SHE MUST
BE SWEET . . .

. . . AND MAYBE TOO OLD.
SHE MIGHT HAVE A LIMP.
OR SHE MIGHT HAVE
ACNE, OR POLIO, OR SOMETHING.

IF THE LADY'S JUST AN ASS—
SAY SHE DOTES ON COPS AND G-MEN—
LET'S SUPPOSE SHE'S LOWER CLASS—
HOW'D HE CHOOSE HER OVER ME THEN?

He used to love me.
He used to love me.
He used to love me.
   GOLDBERG. Ah, don't be pathetic.
   SWEETHEART. She's so pathetic.

WIFE.
IS IT HARD TO DECEIVE ME?

NO, JUST BRING A NOTE FROM HOME.
HE COULD JUST AS WELL LEAVE ME;
WHEN HE'S WITH US,
HE'S SOMEWHERE ALONE.

GOLDBERG & SWEETHEART.
YOU'LL BE FINE . . .
    WIFE.
I'LL BE FINE IF HE LEAVES ME.
BUT, I'M SURE HE WON'T.
TROUBLE IS WE DON'T SAY.
BUT I . . .
    GOLDBERG, SWEETHEART & WIFE.
I FELT HIM SLIPPING AWAY.
I FELT HIM DIE IN MY ARMS,
HIS CHARMS
WERE NOT FOR ME.
NO. NO. NO. NO. NO.
HOW
COULD I EVER COMPETE?
THE CAUSE OF ALL HIS LUST
SHE MUST
BE SWEET.

    WIFE.
THE BITCH MIGHT BE DUMB.
SHE MIGHT THINK HE'S KRIS KRINGLE.
AND HONEST.
AND SINGLE.
    SWEETHEART & GOLDBERG.
HE WILL NOT ADMIT THE TRUTH.
    WIFE.
HE THINKS I MIGHT LIKE SURPRISE.
    SWEETHEART & GOLDBERG.
WHY ARE MEN SO DAMN UNCOUTH?
    WIFE.
OH . . .
    ALL.
ALL THEY EVER TELL ARE LIES!

    WIFE.
I FEEL HIM SLIPPING AWAY

I FEEL HIM DEAD IN MY ARMS
HIS CHARMS
ARE NOT FOR ME.
HOW
CAN I EVER COMPETE?
THE CAUSE OF ALL HIS LUST
SHE MUST
BE SWEET . . .

Liar!!!

WHIZZER GOING DOWN (20/21)

(*MARVIN remembers the first time he had sex
with a man. Should be abstracted.*)

MARVIN.
HE HATES MY WIFE.
I HATE HIS FOOD.
HE THINKS I'M RUDE BUT NICE.
I THINK HE'S NICE BUT INDISCREET.
HE THINKS I'M SWEET,
BUT HE TREATS ME KIND OF FUNNY.
I SAY WHIZZER, WHIZZER BROWN.
I SEE WHIZZER, GOING DOWN.

OH WHIZZER, WHIZZER BROWN
ISN'T IT DELIGHTFUL PLAYING EASY?
YES, WHIZZER, WHIZZER BROWN
I CARE.
I FOUND YOUR DOOR.
WE SING OUT MORE
AND MORE
AND MORE
AND MORE
AND MORE NOW.

HE RUBS MY NECK.
I RUB HIS THIGH.
HE ASKS ME WHY I SWEAT.
I ASK HIM WHY HE BITES HIS NAILS.
AND THEN HE TAKES ME IN HIS ARMS
AND THEN HE LIGHTS ANOTHER CIGARETTE.
I SAY WHIZZER, WHIZZER BROWN.
I SEE WHIZZER, GOING DOWN.

OH WHIZZER, WHIZZER BROWN
ISN'T IT DELIGHTFUL PLAYING EASY?
YES, WHIZZER, WHIZZER BROWN
I CARE.
WE SING OUT MORE
AND MORE
AND MORE

AND MORE
AND MORE NOW.
GO WHIZZER
HOW ABOUT WHIZZER.
BREATHE DEEP WHIZZER.
UP AND HE'S GOING DOWN.
    SWEETHEART & GOLDBERG.
GO WHIZZER
HOW ABOUT WHIZZER
BREATHE DEEP WHIZZER
UP AND HE'S GOING DOWN.
    MARVIN.
HE'S ON HIS KNEES
I'M LYING FLAT
JUST LIKE A BAD IDEA.
HE STARTS TO BLOW
I START TO FIGHT.
THE ROOM IS YELLOW AND THE BED IS WHITE.

HE'S GOING DOWN.
I THINK I'LL DIE AWAY.
HE'S GOING DOWN.
I THINK I'LL DIE, DIE, DIE
I SAY WHIZZER . . .
    LADIES.
WHIZZER . . .
    MARVIN.
WHIZZER BROWN.
I SEE WHIZZER . . .
    LADIES.
WHIZZER . . .
    MARVIN.
GOING DOWN.

(*Dance break — with scat vocals*)

    MARVIN.
HE'S GOING DOWN.
    SWEETHEART & GOLDBERG.
HE'S GOING DOWN.

MARVIN.
HE'S GOING DOWN.
SWEETHEART & GOLDBERG.
HE'S GOING DOWN.
MARVIN.
HE'S GOING DOWN.
SWEETHEART & GOLDBERG.
HE'S GOING DOWN.
MARVIN.
GO WHIZZER.
DOWN!
ALL 3. *Down!!*

MARVIN'S GIDDY SEIZURES — Part II (22)

SWEETHEART.
MARVIN WAS A BOY WHO HAD GIDDY SEIZURES
HE WAS LAUGHING ALL THE TIME.
   GOLDBERG.
BUT WHEN HE WAS GROWN
HE GREW OUT OF TOUCH WITH GIDDY FASHION.
   SWEETHEART.
LISTEN TO HIM LAUGH.
   GOLDBERG.
I'M REMINDED OF THE OLD TIMES
'CAUSE AT LAST HE'S GOT PASSION.

   SWEETHEART.
HE'S SICK.
   WIFE.
I'M SICK AT HEART.
   GOLDBERG.
I'M DELIGHTED.
NO I'M NOT.
BUT IT'S BETTER THAN IT WAS.
LET'S RECAPITULATE THE THINGS HE DOES
TO EARN
MY BLESSINGS.

FIRST HE HURTS HIS WIFE
IT'S A GOOD MOVE IF YOU ASK ME
BUT YOU DIDN'T SO I'M QUIET.
THEN HE HURTS HIS CHILD
THAT'S A LESS GOOD MOVE BUT NECESSARY
HONEST I'LL KEEP QUIET.

ONE MORE THING I FORGOT:

   ALL.
MARVIN HAS A SOMETHING
WHICH MOST EVERYBODY NEEDS:
   SWEETHEART.
CALL IT PASSION,
AND DON'T REGRET IT.

WIFE.
MARVIN AND THE BOY
LIVE HAPPILY EVER AFTER.
THAT'S A SICKENING THOUGHT.

LADIES.
TRUE.
MARVIN,
WHAT ARE YOU DOING?

MARVIN.
PARDON ME FOLKS OUT THERE
BUT I'M HAVING A SEIZURE

LADIES.
OH MARVIN
HEY MARVIN

MARVIN.
YES I'M HAVING A SEIZURE TODAY, HEY,
HEY, HEY.

LADIES.
MARVIN'S GIDDY SEIZURES
MARVIN NEEDS LOVE
HE NEEDS LOVE
HE NEEDS LOVE
HE NEEDS LOVE
OOOOOOOOO.

GOLDBERG.
ALL OF US ALIVE
NEED SOMETHING WE CAN LIVE FOR.

SWEETHEART.
I AM WAITING FOR MY SEIZURE.

WIFE.
SHE IS WAITING FOR HER SEIZURE.

GOLDBERG.
GIDDINESS IS GREAT
WHEN IT'S PASSIONATE AND SEXY.

SWEETHEART.
I AM WAITING FOR MY GIDDY SEIZURE.

GOLDBERG.
HIS SAILS WERE SET
HE LOST HIS DIRECTION

AND THE SEA, BLESS ITS HEART,
WAS AWFULLY ROUGH.
MARVIN HAS WAITED QUITE LONG ENOUGH.
IT'S TIME.
SING IT, MARVIN.

MARVIN.
THIS IS WHAT I'M DOING
PARDON ME FOLKS AT HOME
BUT I'M HAVING A SEIZURE.
LADIES.
OH MARVIN.
HEY MARVIN.
MARVIN.
YES I'M HAVING A SEIZURE TODAY
HEY, HEY, HEY
HEY, HEY!

WATCH ME LAUGH.
LADIES.
MARVIN'S GIDDY SEIZURES.
MARVIN.
WATCH ME SCREAM.
LADIES.
MARVIN'S GIDDY SEIZURES.
MARVIN.
I'M COUNTING ON THIS BOY
TO MAKE ME DREAM.
LADIES.
MARVIN'S GIDDY SEIZURES.
ARMS.
MARVIN.
DISAPPEAR.
LADIES.
LEGS.
MARVIN.
DISAPPEAR.
LADIES.
GROIN.
MARVIN.
DISAPPEAR.
LADIES.
KNEES.

MARVIN.
DISAPPEAR.
WHEN MARVIN THROWS THE BEST FIT OF THE YEAR.
    LADIES.
MARVIN'S GIDDY SEIZURES
MARVIN NEEDS LOVE
HE NEEDS LOVE
HE NEEDS LOVE
HE NEEDS LOVE.
OOOOOOOOO.

MARVIN'S GIDDY SEIZURES
MARVIN NEEDS LOVE
HE NEEDS LOVE
HE NEEDS LOVE
HE NEEDS LOVE
OOOOOOOOO.

MARVIN'S GIDDY SEIZURES
MARVIN NEEDS LOVE . . .
    WIFE.
HE NEEDS LOVE
HE NEEDS LOVE
HE NEEDS LOVE
I GOT LOVE
HE NEEDS LOVE
I GOT LOVE . . .

I'M BREAKING DOWN (22A)

(*The WIFE now understands the situation.*)

WIFE.
I'D LIKE TO BE A PRINCESS ON A THRONE.
TO HAVE A COUNTRY I CAN CALL MY OWN.
AND A KING
WHO'S LUSTY AND REQUIRES A FLING
WITH A FEMALE THING.

GREAT . . . MEN WILL BE MEN . . .
LET ME TURN ON THE GAS.
I SAW THEM IN THE DEN
WITH MARVIN GRABBING SOME GUY'S ASS*

OH SURE, I'M SURE, HE'S SURE HE DID HIS BEST.
I MEAN HE MEANT TO BE WHAT HE WAS NOT.
THE THINGS HE WAS ARE THINGS WHICH I FORGOT.
HE'S A QUEEN, I'M A QUEEN,
WHERE IS OUR CROWN?

I'M BREAKING DOWN
I'M BREAKING DOWN
MY LIFE IS SHITTY
AND MY KID SEEMS LIKE AN IDI-
-OT TO ME.
OH NO, THAT'S SICK.
I MEAN HE'S GREAT.
IT'S ME WHO IS THE MATTER
TALKING MADDER THAN THE MADDEST HATTER.

IF I REPEAT ONE MORE WORD
I SWEAR I'LL LOSE MY BRAIN.
WHAT ELSE SHOULD I EXPLAIN?
OH YES, IT'S TRUE I CAN CRY ON CUE
BUT SO CAN YOU.
I'M BREAKING DOWN.

Alternately (the author prefers:)
WITH MARVIN STUCK IN WHIZZER'S ASS.

I'M BREAKING DOWN.
DOWN, DOWN.
YOU ASK ME IF IT'S FUN
TO CRY OVER NOTHING.
IT IS.
I'M BREAKING DOWN.

I THINK IT'S STRANGE BECAUSE THE SEX WAS GOOD.
IT WASN'T GREAT, BUT IT WAS . . . KNOCK ON WOOD . . .
(KNOCK, KNOCK, KNOCK)
SOMETIMES FAIR.
THE TRUTH THOUGH—HE WAS *AU CONTRAIRE*.
YEARS BEFORE HE'D DARE
TO TRY A LITTLE SOMETHING.
NOW, TALKING OF THEN;
TALKING OF WHEN WE MET,
I'D TAKE HIS MOUTH AND FEET
AND MAKE THEM DO—
(*remembering*)
WELL . . . I FORGET.

I THINK IT'S ROTTEN HOW I LATELY FEEL.
IT'S LIKE A NIGHTMARE HOW THIS ALL PROCEEDS.
I HOPE THAT WHIZZER DON'T FULFILL HIS NEEDS.
"DON'T" IS WRONG!
(*to audience:*)
SING ALONG.
(*to herself:*)
WHAT WAS THE NOUN?

I'M BREAKING DOWN.
I'M BREAKING DOWN.
I'LL SOON REDECORATE THESE STALLS
I WANT SOME PADDING ON THE WALLS.
AND ALSO PILLS
(I WANNA SLEEP);
SURE, THINGS WILL PROB'LY WORSEN
BUT IT'S NOT LIKE I'M A HEALTHY PERSON.
I'VE RETHOUGHT MY TALKS WITH MARV
AND ONE FACT DOES EMERGE;
I NEVER LIKED MY CHIN—
SO THAT IS WHY I AM THINKING THIN

AND ON THE BRINK OF BREAKING DOWN.
I'M BREAKING DOWN.
DOWN, DOWN.
I ONLY WANNA LOVE
A MAN WHO CAN LOVE ME . . .
Or like me . . .
Or hold me . . .
Or touch me . . .
Or stand me . . .

MARVIN WAS NEVER MINE.
HE TOOK HIS MEETINGS IN THE BOYS' LATRINE.
I USED TO CRY.
WE'D MAKE A SCENE.
I'D RATHER DIE THAN DRY CLEAN
MARVIN'S WEDDING GOWN.

I'M BREAKING DOWN.
I'M BREAKING DOWN.
IT'S SO UPSETTING HOW I FOUND
THAT WHAT'S RECTANGULAR IS ROUND.
I MEAN IT STINKS.
I MEAN, HE'S . . . QUEER.
(sing-song)
AND ME, I'M JUST A FREAK
WHO NEEDS IT MAYBE EVERY OTHER WEEK.

I'VE RETHOUGHT THE FUN WE'VE HAD
AND ONE FACT DOES EMERGE:
I PLAYED THE FOOLISH CLOWN.
THE ALMOST-VIRGIN WHO SINGS THIS DIRGE
IS ON THE VERGE
OF BREAKING DOWN.
I'M BREAKING DOWN.
DOWN, DOWN.
THE ONLY THING THAT'S BREAKING *UP*
IS MY MARRIAGE.

THE ONLY THING THAT'S BREAKING *UP*
IS MY MARRIAGE
BUT ME, I'M BREAKING DOWN.
DOOOOOOOOOOOOWWWWWWWWWWWWNNNNNNNN!!

PACKING UP (23)

(MARVIN is leaving his wife.
While he packs, he sings.)

MARVIN.
PEOPLE MIGHT ASK:
DOES HE FEEL AWFUL?
THAT, AND HAS HE GRIEVED?
HONEST TO GOD,
I DO NOT FEEL AWFUL . . .
A LITTLE UNLAWFUL
BUT
A LOT RELIEVED.

ALSO, I'M SURE—
WHEN THIS THING'S PLAYED OUT,
MY KID'S MADE OUT WELL.
WHIZZER WILL ACT VERY PARENTAL,
COMPLETELY GENTLE,
ABSOLUTELY SWELL.
UNLIKE ME WHO'S AT HIS WORST
WHEN HE LACKS A FEE,
WHIZZER BEATS A BUNT TO FIRST:
I'LL JUST WATCH T.V.
WHIZZER'S STUCK HIMSELF WITH GLUE.
WHIZZER'S LOST HIS MIND.
THOSE WERE THINGS I USED TO DO,
WHICH I'LL LEAVE BEHIND.

FIRST SAY "THANKS," THEN "BYE."
THEN YOU LIE WHAT FUN IT'S BEEN.
OR TELL HER YOUR SIN'S
CALLED HANGING ON.
THEN BE GONE.

HONEST TO GOD
NO ONE'S THE VILLAIN
I'M NOT DRESSED IN BLACK.
SUE ME FOR FRAUD.
SUE ME FOR KILLIN'
A WOMAN UNWILLIN'
TO GET ME OFF HER BACK.

I'M NOT A SAINT
LET'S NOT MINCE WORDS HERE
I'M JUST WHAT I SEEM
MAYBE A PRINCE
UP ON A WHITE MARE
AM I YOUR NIGHTMARE
OR YOUR DREAM?

I MIGHT BORROW MILK. OR MORE.
I MIGHT; TO BEGIN.
IF YOU SEE ME AT YOUR DOOR
SWEAR YOU'LL LET ME IN.

(*Instrumental break.*)

I AM LEAVING . . .
AM I LEAVING?
AM I?

PACK IT UP AND CALL IT QUITS
LIKE GOOD QUITTERS DO
PACK IT UP 'CAUSE THIS WAY SHITS
MAYBE THAT WILL TOO.

PACKING UP A CRAZY WIFE.
PACKED A CRAZY SON.
PACKING UP A CRAZY LIFE.
GOD . . .
WHAT HAVE I
DONE?

BREAKFAST OVER SUGAR (24)

(His wife, understanding everything,
wants him to stay. MARVIN wants to go.
Or MARVIN wants to stay. She wants him to go.
Anyway, nothing's resolved: He's going.)

WIFE.
PASS THE SUGAR PLEASE.
I DREAMT LAST NIGHT WE FLEW TO CHINA.
YOUR PARENTS OWN A CAR,
DON'T THEY?
CAN'T WE DRIVE AWAY?   MARVIN.
                                        THE SUGAR PLEASE.
MAY WE TALK AS   PLEASE.
   FRIENDS?
I DREAMT LAST NIGHT   JEEZ-US CHRIST
YOU ALMOST HELD ME   YOU'LL COME THROUGH
I CRY AS IF ON CUE
HOLD ME
HOLD HIM TOO
BUT STAY. (STAY.)

                                        PLEASE
PLEASE DRINK   DRINK YOUR TEA
YOUR TEA   BEFORE IT'S
BEFORE IT'S   COLD.
COLD.

I CAN'T BELIEVE   PASS THE SUGAR
WE'VE   PLEASE.
WORKED   YOU CAN'T GO ON
TO END UP   AS IF YOU'RE DYING
THIS WAY   A MARTYR JUST WON'T
                                           PLAY
                                        HIT ME
STRIP ME DOWN   STRIP ME DOWN
BUT STAY . . .   BUT SAY . . .

PLEASE.   THIS IS MUCH BETTER
                                        FOR THE BOTH OF US.
PLEASE.   NOW THINGS ARE BETTER
                                        FOR THE BOTH OF US.

PASS THE SUGAR
PLEASE.

PASS THE SUGAR ...
PLEASE.

PLEASE.
BOTH.
PLEASE.

PASS THE SUGAR
PLEASE.

PLEASE.
PLEASE.

HIGH SCHOOL SWEETHEART (Reprise) (25)

(*After applause, MISS GOLDBERG enters.*)

GOLDBERG.
GO AHEAD,
PLAY COLUMBUS
STOP BEGGING—
STOP MAKING ME CRAZY, MARVIN
CRAZY MARVIN
I LOVE THE WAY MARVIN ACTS
I DO
DO NOT MAKE FACES
AND DO NOT UNDO THE FACTS:
RELAX. RELAX. RELAX. RELAX.

HOW AMERICA GOT ITS NAME (26)

(an addendum to the Columbus story)

SWEETHEART. When Queen Isabella found out that Columbus was screwing around she was furious. She threw things at him and told him to get out of her country.

GOLDBERG. Isabella was a gutsy woman. People used to lick the streets after she walked by in order to show respect for this great lady. Queen Isabella personally though thought their licking was disgusting — and so do I. But this was Spain, circa 1490, and licking the streets was considered perfectly normal behavior. For the lower classes.

SWEETHEART. As for Columbus . . .

GOLDBERG. Columbus didn't used to be a sailor.

SWEETHEART. From the day he was born, Columbus was slated to be a sailor. Which he became.

GOLDBERG. He was first and foremost a kept man.

SWEETHEART. He was a kept sailor.

GOLDBERG. He did little all day but jot down ridiculous poems and wait for Isabella to call his name.

SWEETHEART. But Queen Isabella, much to her royal displeasure, found out Columbus was cheating on her.

MARVIN. He wasn't cheating exactly.

SWEETHEART. This is what happened. One day — now this is the truth — one day outside Poma del Fuego, he necked furiously with a young man whose red hair and broad shoulders reminded Columbus of his mother. Columbus had never felt such stirrings of deep emotion beneath his Italian marble facade. They met at odd hours off and on for three weeks, Columbus and this gentleman from Poma de Fuego.

GOLDBERG. And soon Isabella, who was no dummy, realized that Columbus was having an affair with someone else.

SWEETHEART. And Columbus had hell to pay, yes sir, and I mean hell.

GOLDBERG. He was out of his mind with grief about Isabella's anger because Isabella paid for his fine clothes, she provided him with a fine apartment, rent-free . . .

MARVIN. And he loved her.

GOLDBERG. You're telling me he grieved because he loved her?

MARVIN. I'm telling you . . .

GOLDBERG. Ah shut up. She wanted him out of her sight — and

the lady always got what she wanted. Isabella swore he would never have another woman as long as he lived, so she put him on a doomed boat with known homosexuals, and laughed a wicked royal laugh.

SWEETHEART. Like this: ha-ha-ha.

GOLDBERG. Those who knew him well say that Columbus was half insane by the time they strapped him to a ship and pushed him out to sea.

MARVIN. On board, Columbus stayed in his room and sulked. He spoke to no one except the porter. He told his porter that if they came across any new land it was to be called Isabella in hopes the Queen would forgive him.

SWEETHEART. He wrote her love letters begging her forgiveness. He wrote:

MARVIN. Dear Isabella, forgive me.

GOLDBERG. You think she was moved? You think so? Then you didn't know Isabella. She laughed in his face.

SWEETHEART. Like this: ha-ha-ha.

GOLDBERG. He wrote her:

MARVIN. Dear Isabella; You don't know the whole story. I was not having an affair with a lady in waiting . . .

SWEETHEART. He would send the letters by carrier pigeon.

GOLDBERG. He wrote:

MARVIN. Dearest Isabella.

SWEETHEART. She laughed in his face.

GOLDBERG. He wrote her:

MARVIN. If I discover any new land, I shall name it Isabella-land.

GOLDBERG. Until one day . . .

SWEETHEART. (This is a love story)

GOLDBERG. There was a knock at the door . . .

SWEETHEART. Of Columbus' room . . .

GOLDBERG. Onboard this ship . . .

SWEETHEART. On which Isabella . . .

GOLDBERG. Royalty of Spain . . .

SWEETHEART. Had deported her kept man . . .

GOLDBERG. Christopher Columbus.

MARVIN. Please come in.

SWEETHEART. Columbus could not believe his eyes.

GOLDBERG. Columbus could not trust his legs.

SWEETHEART. There, outlined by the light of the sea, stood the handsome young man from Poma del Fuego.

MARVIN. Please come in.

GOLDBERG. The young man asked if he could sit down. He asked if there was anything to drink. He asked if he could take off his clothes.

MARVIN. Columbus could not trust his voice.

SWEETHEART. They got into bed.

GOLDBERG. Where they didn't sleep.

MARVIN. We slept a little.

GOLDBERG. For thirty days.

SWEETHEART. Fifty days.

GOLDBERG. 85 rapturous days and nights.

SWEETHEART. When Marvin suggested . . .

MARVIN. Not a moment too soon . . .

SWEETHEART. That they should take a shower — which, thank God, they did.

ALL. All of this Columbus wrote in a letter to Isabella.

GOLDBERG. To tell you the truth, Queen Isabella wasn't interested. She ripped up the letter. She said she was disgusted and appalled. She told her husband that as far as she was concerned, Columbus was one dead explorer.

SWEETHEART. The two bachelors left Columbus' room arm in arm bound for the shower, and were halted by the sight of a magnificent land mass up ahead. Everybody was yelling:

GOLDBERG & SWEETHEART. "Thar's Isabellaland!"

MARVIN. Because that was the name I had told the porter to call any new land we came across.

GOLDBERG & SWEETHEART. "Thar's Isabellaland!"

MARVIN. It was a bright green land.

GOLDBERG. A ballsy land.

SWEETHEART. A land brimming with possibilities.

MARVIN. Men . . .

GOLDBERG. . . . He said . . .

SWEETHEART. He spoke to the assembled homosexuals.

GOLDBERG. He was very moved by this discovery . . .

MARVIN. . . .No longer do I call this Isabellaland. But, rather, this fine green beautiful land I see today, I name America — after Amerigo Vespucci — a young man I met in Poma del Fuego with red hair and broad shoulders like my mother.

ALL.
GOD BLESS AMERICA
GOD BLESS AMERICA
GOD . . .

MARVIN. I love you.

ALL.
HEY, I LOVE YOU
SET THOSE SAILS
A GOOD MAN NEVER FAILS.
HEY, I LOVE YOU
SET THOSE SAILS
A GOOD MAN NEVER . . .

MARVIN. The thing about explorers is: they discover things that are already there. Columbus signed his last letter "Love, Christopher"—and went ashore.

(*MARVIN leaves.*)

BEEN A HELLUVA DAY (REPRISE) (27)

WIFE.
BEEN A HELLUVA DAY
FULL OF MANY SURPRISES.
IT'S TAKEN ALL OF MY WILL
TO STILL STAND HIGH.
MARVIN WROTE ME GOODBYE.
FILLED IT WITH DETAILS.
EXPLICIT THINGS THAT I CAN'T TRY.
SAYS A GOOD MAN NEVER FAILS.
BUT ME—
I LET THE CARDS FALL WHERE THEY MAY.

TIME TO WAKE UP
TIME TO WAKE UP, MARVIN.

TIME I WOKE UP,
AND FACED THE DAY . . .

ANOTHER SLEEPLESS NIGHT (28)

ALL.
ANOTHER SLEEPLESS NIGHT AT HOME IN BED
ANOTHER SILENT DAWN
YOU TRY TO THINK OF THINGS YOU MIGHT HAVE SAID
YOU TRY TO CARRY ON.

SWEETHEART.
I WASH MY FACE
THEN DRINK BEER
THEN I WEEP
SAY A PRAYER AND INDUCE
INSINCERE SELF-ABUSE
TILL I'M FAST ASLEEP.

GOLDBERG.
I'VE DONE TOO MUCH TALKING.
THAT WAY I DON'T LISTEN.
THAT WAY I CAN'T HEAR WHAT YOU MIGHT SAY.
OH, LOOK WORLD WHAT I'VE FOUND
MY EYES ARE GREY AND THE WORLD IS ROUND.

MARVIN.
HE NEVER STOPS,
THIS WHIZZER BROWN.
I NEED MY SLEEP.
FIVE TIMES A NIGHT
HE'LL REQUEST IT;
I WANNA REST IT.
(IT WILL KEEP.)
ALL HE WANTS – WHAT HE WANTS
IS A BODY THAT WON'T FUSS.
SO WE SLEEP IN A BED
TOO BIG FOR TWO PEOPLE.
IT'S BIG FOR TWO PEOPLE
BUT THIS BED IS BIGGER THAN BOTH OF US.
LADIES.
BORED,
BORED,
MARVIN.   LADIES.
I'M FEELING HOT.   BORED,

HE'LL CLOSE HIS EYES	BORED,
AND THEN SURPRISE:	
I'LL BE AWAKE AND PERFORMING.	BORED,
HE'LL WANNA SLEEP	BORED,
BUT ASKS FOR MORE.	
TO PUT UP	BORED,
WITH A GUY	
LIKE MYSELF	
MUST BE A BORE.	BORED.

BUT HE SLEEPS IN THIS BED
WITH ME, A SURVIVOR,
I'M FEELING ALIVE-ER
THAN I'VE EVER FELT IN MY LIFE BEFORE.

ALL.
ANOTHER SLEEPLESS NIGHT AT HOME IN BED.
THE SUN WILL FLY AND DOES
ANOTHER BOOK YOU THOUGHT WAS BEST UNREAD
HAS PROVED INDEED IT WAS.

WIFE.
I BREAK A CUP.
GOLDBERG.
SCAN A POEM.
SWEETHEART.
THEN I EAT.
MARVIN.
SHOWER UP.
SWEETHEART.
STRIKE A POSE.
GOLDBERG.
COUNT MY FEET.
WIFE.
COUNT MY TOES.
MARVIN.
TILL I'M FAST ASLEEP.

ALL.
FAST ASLEEP.
SWEETHEART.
ASLEEP.

WIFE.
NO ONE HERE TO KICK IN BED
NO ONE HERE TO REST MY HEAD AGAINST
I AM SO ALONE
IN THE MIDDLE OF THE NIGHT.

WIFE.
I AM SO ALONE.
SWEETHEART.
I AM SO ALONE.
GOLDBERG.
I AM SO ALONE.
WIFE.
I AM SO ALONE.
ALL.
IN THE MIDDLE OF THE NIGHT.

(*Music.*)

NIGHT.
NIGHT.
NIGHT.

GOODNIGHT (NO HARD FEELINGS) (29)*

MARVIN.
GOODBYE.
GOODBYE TO THE LADIES.
THE DRAMA'S BEEN PLAYED AND NO ONE'S DIED.
PUT OUR PAST ASIDE, AND LOOK AHEAD.
FORGET WHAT I'VE DONE.
AND THINK OF YOURSELVES INSTEAD.

SWEET DREAMS,
BE OFF, AND GOODBYE NOW.
MY CONSCIENCE HAS FINALLY BEEN CLEARED.

IN MY ARMS I FEARED
YOU'D STAND ALONE.
I SWORE I WOULD NOT AGAIN,
NOT VISIT WITH OTHER MEN,
OKAY, SO I LIED, BUT THEN
I'VE GROWN
I'VE GROWN.

LADIES.
ONE LAST WORD BEFORE WE GO.
ONE LAST APPROPRIATE THOUGHT:
GOLDBERG.
YOU DON'T DESERVE WHAT YOU GOT
AT ALL.

SWEETHEART.
NO HARD FEELINGS.
NO HARD FEELINGS, MARVIN.

GOLDBERG.	SWEETHEART.
NO HARD FEELINGS.	NO
NO HARD FEELINGS,	HARD
MARVIN.	FEELINGS.

---

*This song may, if desired, be replaced with "IN TROUSERS – REPRISE (THE DREAM)," which follows.

WIFE.
THINK OF US FROM TIME TO TIME
WE BOTH COMMITTED NO CRIME
YOU GO YOUR WAY, I'LL GO MINE.
    LADIES.
OKAY?

GOLDBERG.	SWEETHEART.	
NO HARD FEEL-INGS	NO	
NO HARD FEEL-INGS,	HARD	
MARVIN,	FEELINGS	
		WIFE.
NO HARD FEEL-INGS	NO HARD	NO HARD
NO HARD FEEL-INGS,	FEELINGS	FEELINGS
MARVIN,		
NO HARD FEEL-INGS	NO HARD	NO HARD
NO HARD FEEL-INGS,	FEELINGS	FEELINGS
MARVIN,		
NO HARD FEEL-INGS	NO	NO
NO HARD FEEL-INGS,	HARD	HARD
MARVIN,	FEELINGS	FEELINGS
MARVIN'S GIDDY SEIZURES	MARVIN'S GIDDY SEIZURES	MARVIN'S GIDDY MARVIN'S GIDDY SEIZURES
MARVIN NEEDS LOVE		
HE NEEDS LOVE	MARVIN'S GIDDY SEIZURES	MARVIN'S GIDDY MARVIN'S GIDDY SEIZURES

    LADIES.
HE NEEDS LOVE
HE NEEDS LOVE
HE NEEDS . . .
    MARVIN.
GOODBYE.
GOODBYE TO THE LADIES.

(*His Wife looks at him, looks away, kisses the shoulder of his bathrobe, leaves.*)

MARVIN.
AT NIGHT I SLEEP LIKE A BABY.
OR MAYBE I WILL AS TIME MOVES ON.
IT'S A SWEET NEW DAWN
ALL COLORED BRIGHT.
MAYBE THERE'S HELL TO PAY,
I'LL PAY IT ANOTHER DAY,
NOW TURN OFF THE LIGHTS,
AND SAY
GOODNIGHT.
GOODNIGHT.

(*The lights fade.*)

"WHIZZER" BOWS (30)
EXIT MUSIC (31)

IN TROUSERS – REPRISE (THE DREAM) (Alternate 29)

(*The author prefers this ending.*)

MARVIN.
FOUR YOUNG LADIES SAT AROUND
  AND SAID THEY'D NEVER LOSE THEIR LOVE.
AND THEN THEY LOST THEIR LOVE.
FIVE GOOD MEN IN TROUSERS
  BANGED A TABLE WHEN THEY'D FOUND THEIR VOICE.
IT WAS A LADIES' CHOICE.
THE WOMEN SAT DEMURE
  AND WHISTLED THROUGH THEIR TEETH;
THEY GAVE DIRECTIONS UNDERNEATH
ON LEGS AND KNEES, THESE
FOUR YOUNG LADIES SAT AROUND
  AND SAID THEY'D NEVER LOSE
THEIR LOVE.
AND THEN THEY LOST THEIR LOVE.

JESSIE WORE A BONNET, MAY A SASH
  WITHOUT A DASH OF CHARM.
AND SIS READ *COMMONWEAL*.
BETTE WAS NERVOUS SO SHE PICKED A SCAB
  FROM SOMEONE ELSE'S ARM.
THEN JESSE BLEW HER MEAL.
THEY HAD A LAUGH, THESE WOMEN
  LAUGHED THEIR VERY BEST.
THE MEN IN TROUSERS AREN'T IMPRESSED.
OR ELSE THEY'RE LAZY.
FOUR YOUNG LADIES SAT AROUND
  AND SAID THEY'D NEVER LOSE THEIR LOVE.
FOUR YOUNG LADIES SAT AROUND
  AND SAID THEY'D NEVER LOSE THEIR LOVE.
FOUR YOUNG LADIES SAT AROUND
  AND SAID THEY'D NEVER LOSE THEIR LOVE.
AND THEN THEY LOST THEIR LOVE.

LADIES.
BABA DUP BA DUP BA DUP BA DUP
BABA DUP BA DUP BA DUP BA DUP
BA DA DA . . .

BABA DUP BA DUP BA DUP BA DUP
BABA DUP BA DUP BA DUP BA DUP
BA DA DA . . .

MARVIN.
WOMEN SIT LIKE ANGELS,
  MEN LIKE VULTURES,
  IT'S A TRIFLE CRUDE.
IT TENDS TO MAKE ONE THINK.
SAME FOLK ACTING LIKE FROM DIFFERENT CULTURES
  AS THEY CHEW THEIR FOOD,
COMPLETELY OUT OF SYNC.
IT'S SIMPLY THIS: FOUR WOMEN
  AND FIVE MEN WON'T MEET.
THEY MUST, FOR LOVE, REMAIN DISCREET—
AND WHO'S TO BLAME THEM?

GOLDBERG.
MARVIN'S GIDDY
  SEIZURES.
MARVIN NEEDS LOVE.
HE NEEDS LOVE,
HE NEEDS LOVE,
HE NEEDS LOVE,
HE NEEDS LOVE.   SWEETHEART.
MARVIN'S GIDDY   MAR . . .
  SEIZURES.
MARVIN NEEDS LOVE. VIN's
HE NEEDS LOVE,   GIDDY   WIFE.
HE NEEDS LOVE,   SEIZURES . . . MARVIN
HE NEEDS LOVE,   NEEDS
                               LOVE.
HE NEEDS LOVE.   LOVE.
MARVIN'S GIDDY   MAR . . .   LOVE.
  SEIZURE
MARVIN NEEDS LOVE. VIN'S
HE NEEDS LOVE,   GIDDY
HE NEEDS LOVE,   SEIZURES . . . MARVIN
HE NEEDS LOVE,   NEEDS
                               LOVE.
HE NEEDS LOVE.   LOVE.
AHH!   AHH!   LOVE!

MARVIN.
JESSE WORKS THE CORNER
  NEAR THE DRUGSTORE,
MAY'S A SOUVENIR
  LEFT ON THE BATHROOM SHELF.
BETTE WEARS FRAGRANCES LIKE
  "*EAU DE WANTING MORE*"
WHILE SIS DRANK BEER,
  AND WENT AND KILLED HERSELF.
I WAS A YOUNG MAN ONCE,
  IN TROUSERS, ONE OF FIVE.
I WRITE TO KEEP THE PAIN ALIVE.
  BUT ASK NO QUESTIONS.
FOUR YOUNG LADIES SAT AROUND
  AND SAID THEY'D NEVER LOSE THEIR LOVE.
FOUR YOUNG LADIES SAT AROUND
  AND SAID THEY'D NEVER LOSE THEIR LOVE.
FOUR YOUNG LADIES SAT AROUND
  AND SAID THEY'D NEVER LOSE
THEIR LOVE.
AND THEN THEY LOSE THEIR LOVE.
  LADIES.
BABA DUP BA DUP BA DUP BA DUP
BABA DUP BA DUP BA DUP BA DUP
BA DA DA . . .
  MARVIN.
AND THEN THEY LOST THEIR LOVE.

  LADIES.
BABA DUP BA DUP BA DUP BA DUP
BABA DUP BA DUP BA DUP BA DUP
BA DA DA . . .

  MARVIN.
BECAUSE WE'RE DREAMING IN TROUSERS,
LAUGHING IN TROUSERS,
PLAYING IN TROUSERS,
MAKING MUSIC IN TROUSERS,
MAKING MOVIES IN TROUSERS,
PEOPLE FIGHTING IN TROUSERS,
PEOPLE SINGING AND DANCING AND
  WRITING IN TROUSERS,

PEOPLE WAITING IN TROUSERS,
PEOPLE CRYING IN TROUSERS,
PEOPLE LIVING IN TROUSERS,
PEOPLE SCREWING IN TROUSERS,
IN TROUSERS, IN TROUSERS,
IN TROUSERS.
IN TROUSERS.

BECAUSE WE'RE DREAMING IN TROUSERS,
LAUGHING IN TROUSERS,
PLAYING IN TROUSERS,
MAKING MUSIC IN TROUSERS,
MAKING MOVIES IN TROUSERS,
PEOPLE FIGHT IN TROUSERS,
PEOPLE SINGING AND DANCING AND
   WRITING IN TROUSERS,
PEOPLE WAITING IN TROUSERS,
PEOPLE CRYING IN TROUSERS,
PEOPLE LIVING IN TROUSERS,
PEOPLE SCREWING IN TROUSERS,
IN TROUSERS, IN TROUSERS,
IN TROUSERS.
IN TROUSERS.

(*The lights fade.*)